Amazing World of Butterflies and Moths

Written by Louis Sabin

Illustrated by Jean Helmer

Troll Associates

Library of Congress Cataloging in Publication Data

Sabin, Louis.
    Amazing world of butterflies and moths.

    Summary: Briefly describes the life cycle of the
butterfly and moth.
    1. Butterflies—Juvenile literature.   2. Moths—
Juvenile literature.   [1. Butterflies.   2. Moths]
I. Helmer, Jean Cassels.   II. Title.
QL545.S23   595.78   81-7504
ISBN 0-89375-560-5   AACR2
ISBN 0-89375-561-3 (pbk.)

The summer sun shines down on fields and flowers. Gracefully, a butterfly lands on a flower. A moment later, it is in the air again, flying to another flower.

It is a warm summer night. A street lamp lights the darkness. Many white and brown insects flutter around the bright light. These insects are moths.

4

Butterflies and moths have been on the Earth for millions of years. These winged insects lived in the time of dinosaurs and saber-toothed tigers. That is much longer than people have lived on the Earth.

Most moths and butterflies live everywhere in the world except in the very coldest places.

In the autumn, the weather grows cool, and the leaves start to fall. Some butterflies and moths fly away. Like many birds, they fly far to the warm south.

Some butterflies and moths do not fly south for the winter. They hibernate, or sleep, during cold weather. One of these is the angle wing butterfly. This insect is the same color as dry leaves. When the weather grows cold, it finds a warm place under some leaves. There it stays, safe and asleep, all winter long.

Most butterflies and moths do not live very long. When cold weather comes, they die. But they have already laid their eggs. These eggs will hatch, and there will be new butterflies and moths next year.

Butterfly and moth eggs are hard to see—they are about the size of the head of a pin. Butterflies and moths lay large numbers of eggs on twigs, leaves, or on the ground. Soon, the eggs hatch. But it is not a winged insect that comes out of each egg. It is a very small caterpillar.

There are all kinds of caterpillars. Some are green. Others are blue or brown. There are striped caterpillars. There are caterpillars with bright dots. Some have smooth skin. Some have skin that is bumpy or furry.

When a caterpillar comes out of its egg, it begins to eat leaves. The caterpillar eats and eats. The more it eats, the bigger it grows. Soon, it is too big for its skin. The skin splits open from front to back.

Out crawls the caterpillar, wearing a new skin. This change of skin is called *molting*. Molting does not hurt the caterpillar. Each time a caterpillar molts, it is much bigger than before.

The caterpillar will molt four or five times before it is fully grown. Then it stops eating. It rests for a few hours. Next, the caterpillar spins out a silk thread from a small knob or bump just below its mouth.

A caterpillar uses its silk thread to build a house. This house is called a *cocoon*. The cocoon is attached to a twig or is hidden in a rolled-up leaf. When the cocoon is finished, the caterpillar is snug inside.

Inside the cocoon, the caterpillar is changing. It becomes a moth. Here is what happens. The caterpillar wiggles out of its old skin. Now its body is covered by a new, hard skin. It looks like a large, brown peanut.

The moth is growing inside the hard, brown skin. Four small wings form. New eyes and feelers grow. There are six thin legs folded close to the body.

When all the changes are done, the caterpillar is gone. In its place is a young moth.

The moth comes out of its shell. It looks like a worm with little wings. It begins to wave its wings and move around. The moth is not able to fly yet.

Each time the moth moves, it sends blood into the veins of its wings. Soon, the moth's wings grow bigger. The body grows smaller. In a short while, the moth is fully grown and ready to fly.

Not all caterpillars turn into moths. Some turn into butterflies. Butterfly caterpillars do not spin cocoons. Instead, they attach themselves to a twig by a single thread of silk. The thread keeps the caterpillar from falling to the ground.

A hard skin, like a shell, forms around the butterfly caterpillar. This skin may be the same color as the twig. Or it may shine silver or gold. When the butterfly comes out of its shell, it pumps up its wings with blood. Once the wings are large and strong enough, it flies away.

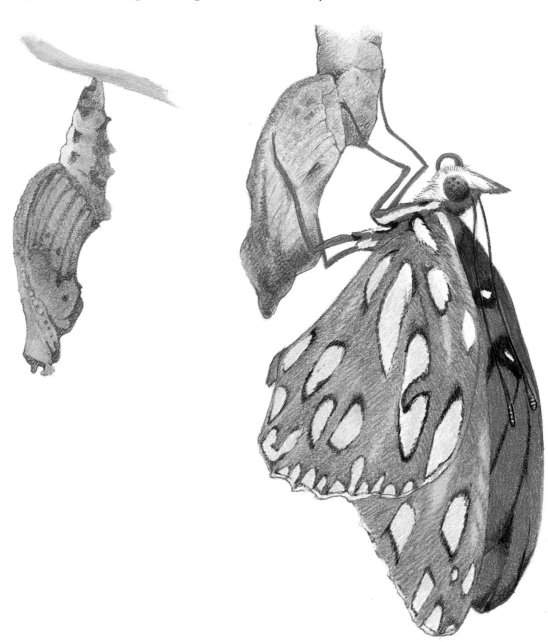

Moths and butterflies look alike, but there are a few ways to tell them apart. Both moths and butterflies have feelers, called *antennae* (an-*teh*-nee). But their antennae are not the same. The antennae of a butterfly are long and thin and have a bump at the end. The antennae of a moth are thicker and have little hairs growing on them.

Swallowtail Butterfly

Butterflies and moths can also be told apart by the way they hold their wings. When a butterfly rests, it holds its wings straight up and close together. When a moth rests, it folds its wings down or spreads them like a bird that is flying.

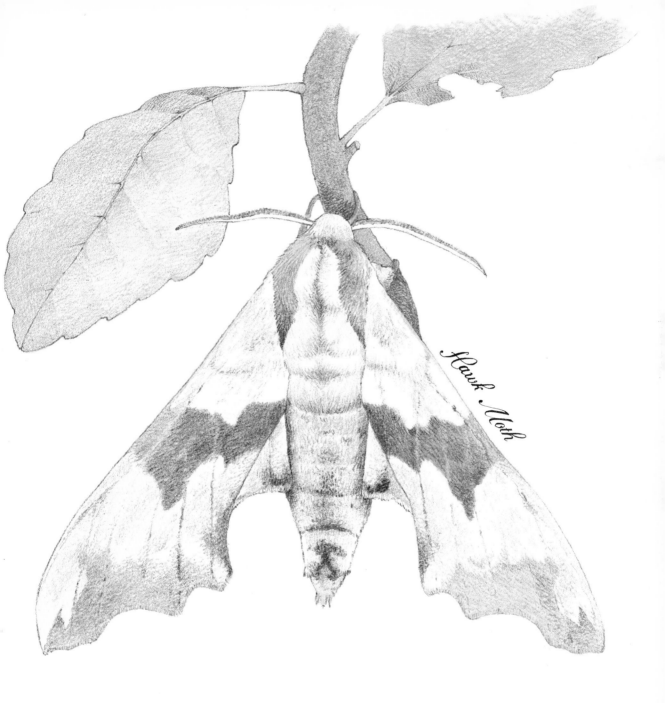

Hawk Moth

There is another difference between butterflies and moths. The butterfly has a long, thin body. The moth's body is thick, and it may also be covered with hair.

Both butterflies and moths drink a sweet liquid called *nectar*. They find it in flowers. They drink it through a long, hollow tongue called a *proboscis* (pro-*bahs*-iss).

When the proboscis is not being used, the moth or butterfly keeps it rolled up under its head. When it wants to drink, the insect stretches out the proboscis, using it the way we use a straw.

The eyes of these beautiful, winged insects are very large. Moths and butterflies can see moving things and colors very well. But they cannot see very far away.

If you touch the wing of a butterfly or moth, you will find that a kind of "dust" comes off it. This dust is really many, many tiny scales. They cover the wings the same way fish scales cover a fish.

All the colors of the rainbow can be seen on the scales of butterflies and moths. Without scales, the wings are very thin and as clear as glass.

The scales also make the wings strong. Like the feathers of a bird, they catch the air and help the insect to fly easily and gracefully.

Millions of caterpillars hatch every year. Sometimes they can be terrible pests. Caterpillars eat the leaves on many small plants and trees. They also eat holes in fruits and vegetables.

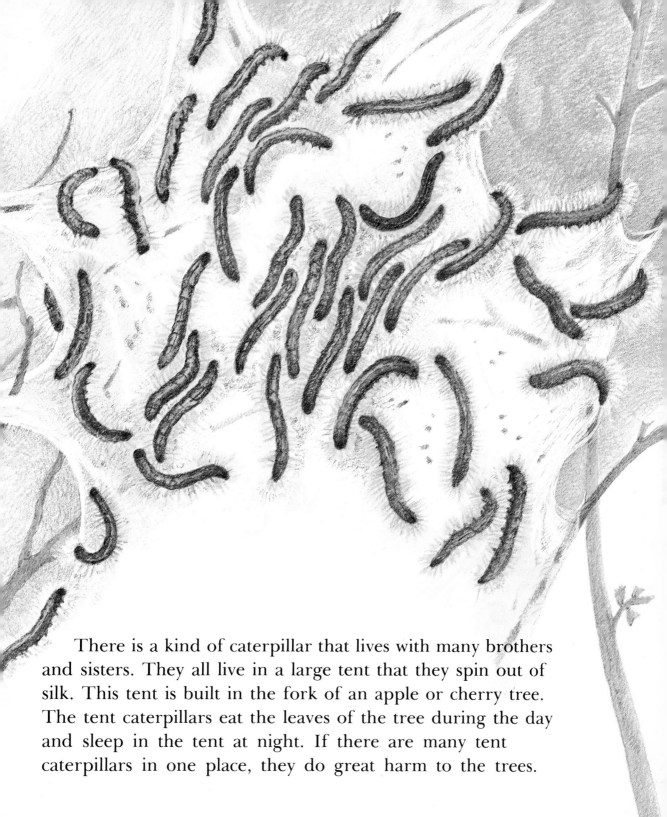

There is a kind of caterpillar that lives with many brothers and sisters. They all live in a large tent that they spin out of silk. This tent is built in the fork of an apple or cherry tree. The tent caterpillars eat the leaves of the tree during the day and sleep in the tent at night. If there are many tent caterpillars in one place, they do great harm to the trees.

Luckily, birds and bats help to keep down the number of harmful caterpillars and moths. Fully grown butterflies are also food for birds. But not all kinds of butterflies get eaten. The pretty orange-and-black monarch butterfly tastes bad to birds. The birds learn this and do not chase the monarch.

Although some caterpillars, moths, and butterflies are harmful, many of these creatures are also helpful. Butterflies and moths help plants to grow, as they fly from flower to flower, looking for nectar. As a butterfly lands on a flower, some of the sticky *pollen* in the center of the flower rubs off onto its legs. When the insect flies to another flower, some of the pollen from the first flower brushes off the insect's legs onto the second flower. The pollen helps to make new plants grow.

Butterflies and moths play an important part in nature. Whether big or small, these insects are always beautiful creatures. And their amazing change from caterpillar to butterfly or moth makes them one of nature's most special groups of insects.

5266